Topsoil
Road

p o e m s

Topsoil Road

ROBERT MORGAN

Louisiana State University Press   *Baton Rouge* MM

First printing
09 08 07 06 05 04 03 02 01 00
5   4   3   2   1

Designer: Amanda McDonald Scallan
Typeface: Janson Text
Printer and binder: Thomson-Shore, Inc.

Library of Congress Cataloging-in-Publication Data

Morgan, Robert, 1944–
  Topsoil Road : poems / Robert Morgan.
    p. cm.
  ISBN 0-8071-2612-8 — ISBN 0-8071-2613-6 (pbk.)
  I. Title.

PS3563.O87147 T66 2000
811'.54—dc21

                                          00-044390

The author gratefully acknowledges the editors of the following journals, in which some of the poems herein first appeared, sometimes in slightly different form: *American Scholar, Atlantic Monthly, Banyan, Carolina Quarterly, Chiaroscuro, Christian Science Monitor, DoubleTake, Epoch, Georgia Review, Graham House Review, Image, Kenyon Review, Michigan Quarterly Review, Now & Then, Paris Review, Poetry, St. Andrews Review, Shenandoah, Southern Review, Virginia Quarterly Review, William and Mary Review.*

"Care" was published as a broadside in 1998 by the North Caroliniana Society of the University of North Carolina at Chapel Hill. "History's Madrigal" was published as a broadside in 1999 by Robert Denham at the Melas Press in Salem, Virginia.

Many of these poems first appeared in the chapbook *Wild Peavines* (Gnomon Press, 1996). Special thanks to Jonathan Greene.

Thanks also to Roger Gilbert, Michael Mcfee, and Robert West for reading this book in manuscript. Their suggestions have been invaluable.

For my daughter Katie

Contents

Two

One

Attakullakulla Goes to London

How dry the English seemed, their skin
unrubbed, ungreased, their hair undressed
with bear's oil and covered by gray
wigs so each looked old and wise.
They even put on powder to
smother any redness so each
face looked chalky as a corpse.
At Whitehall he drank a thimble
of sherry and heard the gentle
talk of war, and knelt before the great
wise Chief, offering the crown of
five eagle tails, then put on silks
for church. And lying in the cold
white bed in the tavern room both
government and governor refused
to pay for, sore from standing hours
to have a portrait, the Little
Carpenter, smallest and quickest
chief, dreamed of blue mountains across
the hilly ocean, beyond Charleston
and the forts, up the Estatoe
Trail, past middle and upper towns,
where on a single chestnut prong, a bear
was tearing open wood to get
the heart of honey, and every
bee raked out with the mushy sweet
mess and blurring in surprise
had the wet and oil-bright face
of some familiar Cherokee.

Signal Fires

At Long Rock you still see the holes
made by fires the Cherokees lit
there, now pots filled with rain like
cisterns, where the bonflames roared as
messages sent mountaintop to
mountaintop all the way from first
foothills to Pinnacle on to
Pisgah, to the Smokies and into
Tennessee. Every flat rock
on a summit was the site for
signaling, the high fires reaching
through dark farther and clearer
than drums or smoke could, faster than
the quickest runner, as light answered
light from ridge to distant ridge,
one lit pile touching off the echo
of another in a chain that called
to war or ball-play, or warned of
invasion, or marked a mighty
celebration through scattered towns,
the mountains tipped articulate
above the tangled trails and creeks,
across black and multiplying peaks.

Topsoil Road

The first wagon trace into hills
took no grading. A few trees cut
and brush knocked down or pushed aside,
the route went right across the ridge
and down along the branch. Wheels sliced
into leaves and tore the humus,
banged on roots and rocks and ground
the topsoil in the rush toward
the horizon, to step into
the future the West pulled them to.
No creek or rocky shelf could stall
such exhilaration. Their passion
poured in floods along the ruts as
oxen bawled and stabbed the dirt with
hooves and horses tamped the gravel.
When it rained every track became
a runnel, became a run or
ditch becoming a gully in
yellow clay and red, the wash burned
deep in wet weather reaching to
bedrock and subsoil and making
new horizons in dust as traffic
plowed and plowed again thaw furrows
and puddle holes, until the road
was more pit than passageway, more
obstacle than access, and yet
another must be found to soothe
the unbearable urge to stride
beyond and back, as eros fed
erosion and wander vision
vanished quick as snow in May.

Girdling

Quicker than the felling of trees,
a single ringing of the bark
aboveground opened a wild grove
the first summer of settlement.
As buds dried up, the sap thread cut,
sun touched virgin forest floor.
Corn planted in hills not rows stretched
faster than briars or weeds. Feeding
on centuries of leafmold, the stalks
reached up among the dying limbs
before tasseling. By dog days
the girdled acres brimmed with corn
and nettles, honeysuckle vines.
By the next spring rotting twig-ends
and little branches peppered down
on the plowed ground. And by the third
year whole sheaths of bark dropped like shields
of a defeated army on
the hearth of cultivation. In five
years the standing trunks looked like stones
and statues in a graveyard as
crops rose and fell with the season.
In a decade the woods were gone.

Thrush Doctor

Who knows how the thrush-healer found
out his special gift? How would he
discover he was the chosen,
that just by putting his lips on
a sick baby's mouth and blowing
down the inflamed throat he could cure
that little one? Who'd experiment
with the afflicted to prove his
talent? Yet every community,
each valley, seemed to have one man
with the power, who never failed
when called from field or church or bed
to come and drive away the sickness from
the crying mouth, as though blowing
a soothing note, speaking a charmed
syllable, three times repeated,
put the fever out, and the throat
cooled and the pain vanished after
that peculiar, inspired kiss.

Fever Wit

If a child or young adult lay
near crisis with a temperature,
bedclothes hot as from an iron,
face swollen bright as a blown coal,
neighbors and kin would gather round,
sitting near the bedside, leaning
close, awaiting words uttered from
delirium, the scattered phrase
and mutter from hot throat and brain.
Every mumble seemed a message
to interpret, each groan and wince,
jerk and whisper, a report in
testimony from other tongues,
as though the sick child glowing with
infection could see beyond in
fever intoxication, become
a filament for lighting their
ordinary lives with lightning glimpse
burned through the secret boundary,
the ill one privileged to say
across and not distort or resist
the wisdom of sickness, the vision
from pain-fire's further peaks, before
the dreaded sweat, the chill descent.

Wild Peavines

I have never understood how
the mountains when first seen by hunters
and traders and settlers were covered
with peavines. How could every cove
and clearing, old field, every
opening in the woods and even
understories of deep woods
be laced with vines and blossoms in
June? They say the flowers were so thick
the fumes were smothering. They tell
of shining fogs of bees above
the sprawling mess and every bush
and sapling tangled with tender
curls and tresses. I don't see how
it was possible for wild peas
to take the woods in shade and deep
hollows and spread over cliffs in
hanging gardens and choke out other
flowers. It's hard to believe the creek
banks and high ledges were that bright.
But hardest of all is to see
how such profusion, such overwhelming
lushness and lavish, could vanish,
so completely disappear that
you must look through several valleys
to find a sprig or strand of wild
peavine curling on a weedstalk
like some word from a lost language
once flourishing on every tongue.

7

Sanghoe

Pick for grubbing shiny roots sweet
as a hog's testicles. Far out
on the mountain's spine, over
the jump-off to South Carolina,
you see the berries bright as fire
seeming to float on a tether
after leaves are gone, and under
them the knot and nut and nugget
of potency the Chinese love,
the root powders that warm and rev
old age and thrill the flesh more than
liquor and whip desire and even
heal the black bruise of blues and send
a torch out through the veins and limbs
many-colored as northern lights,
ringing under ordinary dirt.

Outbuildings

First the woodshed with its overhanging
brim and bin of kindling sticks that burn
a cool incense of seasoning. And then
the outhouse with its intimate shadows
off to one side among the pokeweeds, flower beds.
And the chicken house with its floor of acrid
chalk and dusts that crawl in all directions.
The cloth of wire fence hangs behind the clothesline.
The barn shoulders high above the tackle
and gear of the harness room, above the sweet
herbs and shucks of fodder. Beyond the salty
dark of smokehouse and whispery gloom of springhouse,
the chicken coops and hogpen, the tool shed with its
rust assortments, points and dirty planters,
behind the corncrib and molasses shed,
to the final outpost of the homeplace,
on a poplar at the wood's edge, stares
the birdhouse with its one big eye where
unsettled land touches unsettled land.

Blowing Rock

The air that riots up the mountainside
and up the cliff face flames so brusque and bold
it stuns. And what a welling forth, a blaze
of inspiration from the deep ravine.
How could the plain and hollow send a gale
of pentecost prevailing upward with
such wild and steady sharpness? Smell the fumes
of weed and highway, chimney, in the draft.
Wind carries pollen and the breath of woods
it passes over. And the fountain air
feels hard enough to lift a house away
or throw a leaper back onto the ledge.
A hat tossed on the current shoots to heights
above the mountain. What a place to conjure:
the lip of ridge where breath of deep blue valleys
ascends and keeps ascending like a prayer
or song of praise, of supplication, sent
from busy fields and crossways far below
to oracle the towering element.

Squatting

The men in rural places when
they stop to talk and visit will
not stand, for that would make it seem
they're in a rush. Nor will they sit
on ground that might be cold or wet.
Instead they squat with dignity
on heels close to the ground and chat
for hours. And while they tell and answer,
or listen, hunkered out of wind,
they draw with sticks in dirt a map
to illustrate a story or
show evidence for argument.
They sketch out patterns, write on dirt
and doodle vague arithmetic,
who never will take up a pen
on page or slate or canvas. They
will absentmindedly make shapes
and figures of their reveries
and rub them out again complete
to give their art no status of
attention in the casual toss
of discourse, open forum of
community, out there on bare
familiar ground where generations
have squatted, called it ownership.

The Blue Hole

The deepest pool in Green River,
the Blue Hole under Fish-top Falls,
never revealed its depths even
in drought. On brightest days its hue
stayed dark as thunder, still as
memory. Once, every year the eels
appeared here, hundreds of slippery
whips seething. And cove people took
them in nets, with hooks and pitchforks,
took them with dooms of dynamite,
bushels of glistening spawners that
had come back to Green River up
the Broad, up the Pacolet, up
the Cooper, from the Atlantic
all the way from the Sargasso Sea
to trouble waters of this hole
below the falls where they had hatched
as elvers and kept the memory
of the birth waters. The path of
return's now closed by the dam at
Lake Adger, dammed by Lake Moultrie
and Lake Marion, the ancient
long communication broken
between local pool, high ocean.

Care

On a cold morning when our grits,
oatmeal, cream of wheat, were dragon hot,
Daddy would take the threatening plates
out to the back porch and blow at

the smoking porridge. He would pant
the steam away and huff until
we laughed at his choo-chooing chant
to drive away the haunt, expel

the fire ghosts that stung our tongues.
We'd wait for him to bring the dishes
back exorcised by his lungs'
performance of burning frenzies,

by the low notes of his breath-fit,
by the owl calls that hushed heat.

Working in the Rain

My father loved more than anything to
work outside in wet weather. Beginning
at daylight he'd go out in dripping brush
to mow or pull weeds for hog and chickens.
First his shoulders got damp and the drops from
his hat ran down his back. When even his
armpits were soaked he came in to dry out
by the fire, make coffee, read a little.
But if the rain continued he'd soon be
restless, and go out to sharpen tools in
the shed or carry wood in from the pile,
then open up a puddle to the drain,
working by steps back into the downpour.
I thought he sought the privacy of rain,
the one time no one was likely to be
out and he was left to the intimacy
of drops touching every leaf and tree in
the woods and the easy muttering of
drip and runoff, the shine of pools behind
grass dams. He could not resist the long
ritual, the companionship and freedom
of falling weather, or even the cold
drenching, the heavy soak and chill of clothes
and sobbing of fingers and sacrifice
of shoes that earned a baking by the fire
and washed fatigue after the wandering
and loneliness in the country of rain.

Mowing

A summer-long ritual for my father.
Half-dancing and half-rowing into a weed bank,
he gripped the handles of the snath
and swung, beginning high and back, and followed
through, running the blade true
to the ground and then up to winnow
away the cut ends. Snakes and field mice
and my mother's flowers got beheaded
in his rage to mow, and pokeweeds, briars
around the pasture, were subdued to his measure.
He even cut the shoulders of the public road,
exposing beer cans and bags of trash,
and once each season cleaned off the churchyard
and cemetery acre. Mowing met his first requirements:
solitude and no monetary gain. As he swung
he must have seen the heads of neighbors,
deacons, wife and son, topple
and the stubble bleed, for their intrusion
on his long reverie. That blade,
a wide wing of metal, tempered in Czechoslovakia,
soared around and back, making its deadly time
regular as a pendulum, touching its flame
with a hiss to the green stampede.
But there was no end, except frost, to the siege
of tender growth. Suddenly he'd stop
and, holding the scythe upright, take the stone
from his hip pocket and whet the blade brilliant,
spit on his hands and return to the lone war.

I see him there now, wading in rampant vines,
turning quick as a matador in overalls and wrecked hat,
reaching back with his instrument to let
the next wave of summer plunge past and wilt.

Atomic Age

In yards and medians of interstates,
on grounds of factories and hospitals
in Atlanta, Charlotte, Memphis, Nashville,
see patches of Green River soil. For each
boxwood and sparkling pine, every dogwood
and maple from a nursery here, goes with
its ball of mountain dirt to the new bed.
Every rhododendron must keep its roots
in Blue Ridge loam. And while the loam
is scattered in clots of gunpowder black
all over the South, the topsoil in these
mountain coves gets thinner, pocked as sponges,
fissioned to the suburbs, cities, greasy
savings of centuries of leaf rot, forest mold
nursed by summit fogs and isolation,
sold to decorate the cities of the plain.

Heat Lightning

When I was four I was afraid
of any gunshot or backfire
or clap of thunder. I lived in
terror that a rifle crack would
break the sky or crush my own head.
It seemed a firecracker could split
time in two. Big noise was the start
of doom. I lived in fear of cap
guns and the preacher's shouts. Even
the pain of earache was not as
scary as the voice that shadowed
lightning. My mother said I was
awakened at the service for my
soldier uncle by the salute
fired over us and did not forget.
And all the talk of nuclear war
did not soothe me. Each day I saw
all matter crumble from within,
the sky melting in a flash and flesh
boiled by the report of explosions
just over the horizon. Even
heat lightning thrilled me into hiding
as the north lit up, lit up, and
I listened for the whoosh of hell
and awful pain already felt
inside my ears, and waited for
the lethal thrust that never came.

June Bug

With a thread on his claw I flew
my June bug like a model plane
around the hot pasture. It dipped
and circled and looped above me
as I ran to find wind. Over
the steaming grass it dove like
a jeweled fighter tethered to my
finger, then disappeared into
the swarm of its own kind in clover
and indigo. I had to pull it
back to our play, but let it lead
me in compensation over
the meadow. As it swung close to
my ear I felt the tiny wind
from its wings like a love whisper.

Oranges

Not once-a-year gold Christmas
things, as parents recalled, still
oranges were holiday and
maybe ten a winter lights, planets
stuffed bright as pencils in our socks.
Round royal orbs, each weighed a full
goblet. There was no other scent
to rhyme with this, no mix of resin,
flower. The meat and color were
a primary on which comparisons
were based. Daddy carved out a cone
so I could squeeze and drink. One
Christmas morning–I was six–we
carried presents out through cracker
fire and spurs of frost–we the poor
relatives, they never came to us–
to get ours in return. Suddenly
Uncle saw me looking on at
tree and presents heaped all over
the living room, nothing in my
hands, and ran to the fridge to fill
my pockets and arms and grasp with
globes of Persia and Arabia bright
as my (and his) embarrassment.

Vapor Salve

When a fever made time crooked
and light all crossed against itself,
and breath was shrunk to raw choking
on salty fat, Mama got down
the silver tin from the mantel.
The salve looked like greasy ice, smelled
of blizzards from the little can.
She rubbed the resin on my heart,
and I felt at once the needle sting
and thrill of weather soaking through
tight heat. Crusts and dumplings broke.
But what I noticed most were blue
spirits rising from my skin, scents
of pine and gum, a clear ghost swept
out through the air and opening
corridors and bright ledges,
letting in new air and stretching
time like smoke to where it becomes sky.

Besom

With her little bundle of twigs
tied together in a rag my
grandma brushed away the litter
in the yard, painting neatness on
the ground and leaving stroke marks in
the sand and dirt like intended
designs. The space seemed perfect then,
set aside from use, and I stayed
on the grass around the edges,
fearing to step on her lines that
dried white in the sun and almost
disappeared. Then a chicken walked
across the area and plopped
a wet stain down, leaving tracks and
peckholes, and a leaf from the oak
skidded by and caught on a can.
The cat ran across the powdery
patterns, and the spell was shattered
as the traffic resumed on dirt,
as ordinary circulations
blurred her sandscripts, incidental runes.

Companions

In the morning I could tell how
Old Tony felt. When hitched up he
might seem withdrawn, even depressed.
And once in harness he would act
sore from the previous day's work,
or stiff from a night of bad sleep,
and pull into the collar with
reluctance, hesitating at
the turn toward the field. Slower
in the first rows, he slouched ahead
of the cultivator, brushing
the tender bean vines and looking
around as though hoping to be
excused, to call it a day and
return to the pasture. He pulled
without will in a perfunctory
gait, as sun drank the mist on trees
by the river and found the dewy
weeds and vines. Then as he warmed up,
as damp shadows behind clods began
to vanish and only cobwebs
in the stubble sparkled, he loosened
his stride, began to step into
the pull, springing into the work
itself, walking with precision
into the form of the task. And
by midmorning as the air lit
and sweat darkened his coat behind
the collar and under straps, he
attacked the rows ahead in sure

rhythm, the soreness exorcised.
He worked alert to every
nuance of voice and line, turning
without overstepping trace chains,
pulling accurate and straight for yon
end, accommodating ripples
of the vines and irregularities
in rows, the ring of plow on rock,
toward the cool drink from the spring
and grain in his box at noon, freedom
of the green meadow, and the old
companionship with fatigue as
the field darkened clean of weeds.

Polishing the Silver

Even kept inside its closet
the family tea set, candlestick,
will darken in a year, the brightwork
clouding and smudged with soot

oxygen leaves tasting silver
through months of still and darkness.
We bring the stuff to the terrace
and the polish cream in its jar

and rub away the smoke to find
the mirror flesh original
reflecting us in the ritual,
scrubbing till the heirloom's new and

perfect, glitters as when beaten
and brought back from Charleston over
muddy trail and swollen river
and kept hidden like a weapon.

Family Bible

The leather of the book is soft
and black as that of Grandma's purse,
brought west by horse and wagon, kept
on mantel shelf and closet plank.
The red dye on the edge has faded.
The marriages recorded, births
and deaths set down in pencil and
in many inks and hands, with names
and middle names and different dates
and spellings scrawled in berry juice
that looks like ancient blood. And blood
is what the book's about, the blood
of sacrifice, the blood of Lamb,
two testaments of blood, and blood
of families set in names to show
the course and merging branches, roots
of fluid in your veins this moment.
You open crackly pages thin
as film of river birch and read
the law of blood and soar of blood
in print of word and print of thumb.

Translumination

The white sand sprinkled over graves
is gathered from the branch and screened
to get the pebbles out, the sticks
and trash. How bright the mound looks in
the sun, sparkling as though with
sugar or frost, in contrast to
the weeds around, and washed red clay.
The little hill seems more monument
than the rough stone, raised like a reef
or sandbar there to show how shallow
time's waters are, and how we can
almost see through earth, and how pure
death is supposed to be, shining
in the plot like a diamond
shroud hovering, almost blinding.

Hearth

Only the chimney is standing
at the houseplace in the meadow,
fieldstone set on fieldstone, flush,
and scoured by rain and thaw of soot.

At the houseplace in the meadow
grass is rising in the fireplace, lush,
and scoured by rain and thaw of soot.
Licked by wind it leaps off the hearth,

grass rising in the fireplace lush,
and reaches up the chimney's throat;
licked by wind it leaps off the hearth,
kindling in the afternoon sun,

and reaches up the chimney's throat,
bending in the dance of rooted things,
kindling in the afternoon sun.
And bees have found a clover there

bending in the dance of rooted things
where the honey of flames was.
And bees have found a clover there
to sweeten the darkest parlor

where the honey of flames was,
fieldstone set on fieldstone, flush,
to sweeten the darkest parlor.
Only the chimney is standing.

Two

Sharpening a Saw

Any blunt rock can whet a knife
or even scythe blade just by
rubbing the edge at the right pitch,
coaching steel to bright and deadly
thinness. But only a lean hard
file will urge the new edges on
a saw, each tooth with its own
attitude and face to be
flattened, to be caressed to
biting definition. It is
the different angles of the hundred
teeth that make the blade cut fast,
the crystals brushed new and tilted
like little wedges that follow
each other and follow each other
to split the fibers going this
way and coming back, savoring
each crumb of dust, the work done by
prisms no bigger than a line of salt.

Wind from a Waterfall

The air around a waterfall
is thrilling. Gusts and downdrafts prowl
from out of mist and rainbow air
will seem to pour right off the roar.
But take one step and feel the breeze
reverse and veer away in craze
of air around the plunge, perform
a theater of tumbling foam
in knots, a hundred whips and currents,
as tons of milk and spray condense
in atmospheres pushed down that must
escape across the bottom, forced
to circulate as eddies, spin
of backwash, pocket, conflagration.
And as above a witch's cauldron,
the air goes wild and darts, is torn
by fits and swoops of jubilation,
then whispers, barks, in pentecost
and song of families long lost
from far upstream and still stirred up
by heavy tongue from river's lip.

Chicken Scratches

Between packed clay of the center
yard and the weeds and shrubbery,
dirt has been raked and scored, crumbs
drying to meal. Some stylus might
have cut the surface and made
a scrawled hand, the little troughs
intersecting, the scabs of crust
picked loose and fresh-stirred mica
signaling around the water can
and boxwoods and dust-holed bank.
The yard deserted, they seem some
funny ogham fading its script
of quest, where the old cluckers raked
back with one claw and then another,
pecked at seeds and grubs and worm eggs
too fine for bigger eyes to catch
among the chalks and gritty signs,
the incunabula of morning.

Convection

In the stillest house it startles
to see the curtains move above
the radiator, stirred by unseen
fountains, unseen drafts from warmed sweet
metal, showing the air alive
and rising in an oracle,
the lift within each calorie
and molecule, each element,
the fabric troubled by ghosts of
excitement so even emptiness
when touched by heat or pain becomes
breath, becomes aspiration to
convey across the difference change,
the clear trembling flower of haunt.

Heel Taps

What was it about the little half-moon
of metal on the rear of a shoe heel?
All boys in school that year had them.
Nailed just where the rubber wore, the plate rang
a coin on steps and gravel, clinked on floors
to make each step a dance, add percussion
to the strut of walking. And turned up on
a knee the tap shone like a gorget
of honor, a piece of armor to defend
your heel and trample dirt and strike sparks from
grit to celebrate your stride across
the world and make you feel taller by a dime's
worth of the moon's own metal of illusion.

Blizzard

Kudzu has shoaled up the highway
bank, bandaging and sewing clay,
the smocked red folds of subsoil.
Advance lines have thrown and pulled
themselves into the hardwoods, and raised
leaf-tents on dying trunks. The dog days
are now green in a blizzard
of vine-wind and drifts and storm-weird
flattening, leaving the ghosts
of great oaks stooped and almost lost
under the prevailing tempest.
Runners thread deadmen's eyes and seize
the guy wires and creosote prize
of a telephone pole to wrap
in hungry tightness, swarming to the top.
One strand feels out a line, gripping
and searching, as the whole glittering
world is a waste of lushness.

Fulgurite

Where lightning touches sandy soil
exposed on crag or mountaintop
with its blinding tongue, you often
find a glassy rock of fused grains.
The piece looks like a root or tuber,
tubular as wrenched and melted
pottery, a gland or hollow
nugget. The mystery is the hole
through which light shot, evaporating
all but what surrounded it and
leaving us a stencil or mold
of fire's true path long afterward,
leaving us a record of light's
entry of earth, shiny as pipe
or ruined flute or mouthpiece through
which the sky once spoke its sentence
of destructive translation.

Wind Rider

The small zebra spider from its high perch
on post or limb or even joe-pye weed
spits out a floss on the prevailing breeze,
casts like an angler the glimmering thread

until the strand rides out on the zephyr
wafting like a long thrilling melody
over road and yard and narrow valley
to catch and stretch a tightwire bridge.

The spider rows like a high-wire artist
on the milky monofilament from
its own gut. But in a high wind, or from
a higher launch, the quickened air will seize

the silver silk as though it were a sail
and pull it and its author on a long
vowel of wind, soaring on the whip-string
of the spider's effusion, on and on and

farther over fence and shrub and river,
tossed by updrafts and thermals, crosswinds
and eddies, looping in a cadenza
above weeds and chicken yards until

the gossamer one-thread carpet catches
on a twig and the windwalker hangs like
a single bright note on the elastic
of its far-flung transporting syllable.

Music of the Spheres

The first music we don't hear but
know, is inner, the rings around
atoms singing, the bright levels
in matter revealed by colors
through spectrum scales all up and down
the quantum ladder in fireworks
of the inner horizons, each
zone voicing its wavelength with
choirs in the tiny stadiums
of harmony of the deeper
galaxies, ancient octaves
and intervals, lit cities
within every speck of substance.

Π

The secret relationship
of line and circle, progress
and return, is always known,
transcendental and yet
a commonplace. And though
the connection is written
it cannot be written out
in full, never perfect, but
is exact and constant, is
eternal and everyday
as orbits of electrons,
chemical rings, noted here
in one brief sign as gateway
to completed turns and
the distance inside circles,
both compact and infinite.

Snake Fence

A fence will plant a row of trees,
it's said, just like an orchardman
had set them. Birds that rest on rails
or wire or posts do all the work.
And as the fence falls down or rots
and disappears the trees reach up
and march into maturity
in line. But where a snake fence zagged
like splintered lightning through a field
and pinked the edge of pasture lot,
the trees the birds set out are staggered.
The line tacks folded in its stretch
across the ridge or peneplain,
but still articulate where rails
lay angled, meshed with rails this way,
that way, in rhythm and in rhyme
across the open field beneath
the larger measure of the mountains.

Harvest Sink

The quills and pens of summer, pipes
and hollow bones, now shine out to
the edge of golden clouds. The wheat
rolls yellow as the coins of woods.
Where now are the hidden valleys
of rain, covert ditches, the shades
of rusts and mildews, smuts and molds
of early summer? Dry clouds tower
in other brightness. Flames spring out
of corn, from vetch and sicklepod,
thistle. The milk of hay is dust.
The little sugarcanes and money
of grass are gritted roughage. Now
every fat weed has gone to harvest.
The sky is still as farthest mountain.

Crow String

Why a single thread pulled tight
across the corn between saplings
tall as flagpoles will keep away
the crows is anybody's guess.
Perhaps they see the string—their sight
godly sharp—as metonym
for some great net to snare them. Or
maybe the line, strung diagonal
above the rows and glistening
with sun or dew, suggests a zone
in airspace, a boundary to
the lanes above, frustrating flight,
hinting not only of obstacles
but tethers, whips, as the scarecrow
beneath raises its arm throughout
another day and the fine floss
hums its one note of vigil and
alertness in the summer drafts,
heard only by the black watchers
in the pines, eyes bright as new corn.

Manifest

The cobwebs above the china
closet cannot be seen except
from certain angles, or at times
when early sun or late sun pours
almost upward from the windows.
And then the hangings, white trapeze
and nets and hammocks, the tents with
their flannel of dust, shine gold, shine
like vapor trails, like ghost bridges
and smoke flags and fiery tracers
of molecules, the circus of
electrons transfigured up near
the ceiling for a few minutes
of energy revealed. But then
the space above the closet gets
dark again, empty, while the fine
invisible funambulists
and lacemaking sailors go on
about their lofty work, and play,
in eldorados behind each mote.

Bread

When the lushness hangs heavy
in the husk-opening wind
and sheds to blindness, we attend
the gold perfection, sun's lethargy.

On the swept floor the big grass
is beaten for its ripeness;
a fine precipitate
is shoveled on the air to let

wind pluck and choose, its eye do
the fine work. The carats brought
to stone and sharpened into
dust are touched again with water's smart

and the ashes sour whole.
A minute demon conjures in
the mire and breathes it full,
and alchemy's corruptions spin

lace from the dust and breath,
a cloud of flesh woven
from luminous earth
to be healed by fire again and broken.

Amber

Some great pine's finest scab,
this piece of cough drop sucked
by time, warms light, and in
its lens burns ancient resin
to an ember of licked
ice, an ember of fat

caution light. The fly
drowns forever in hard honey.

Oxbow Lakes

The knots tied by a river
become lost ends as the tangles
and meanders separate, cut off
in the streamline of erosion,

become lost ends as the tangles
silt up in dead lakes, fatten
in the streamline of erosion,
old bends not communicating,

silt up in dead lakes, fatten,
left to slime and whisker with sedge,
old bends not communicating
as former drafts and channels green,

left to slime and whisker with sedge,
lost in alluvial succession,
as former drafts and channels green
in the river's variorum,

lost in alluvial succession
as the meanders separate, cut off
in the river's variorum,
the knots tied by a river.

History's Madrigal

When fiddle makers and dulcimer
makers look for best material they
prefer old woods, not just seasoned
but antique, aged, like timbers out
of condemned buildings and poles of
attics and broken furniture
from attics. When asked, they will say
the older wood has sweeter, more
mellow sounds, makes truer and deeper
music, as if the walnut or
cherry, cedar or maple, as
it aged, stored up the knowledge of
passing seasons, the cold and thaw,
whine of storm, bird call and love
moan, news of wars and mourning, in
its fibers, in the sparkling grain,
to be summoned and released by
the craftsman's hands and by careful
fingers on the strings' vibration
decades and generations after
that, the memory and wisdom of
wood delighting air as century
speaks to century and history
dissolves history across the long
and tangled madrigal of time.

Tail Music

When old-time fiddle makers put
a rattlesnake rattle inside
an instrument, they meant to swell
the resonance of the sound box,
give the wood vibrations added
flavor of thresh and shiver-hum
of the serpent's tail-music. But
just the presence of the rattles
must have made the fiddlers feel more
daring, the fiddle dangerous
as the devil's instrument it
was called by deacons and preachers,
the notes hypnotic as a snake's
stare, and stirring evil in young
bodies, the crackle of the rattler's
warning adding to the thrill and
adding to the inclination
to dance all night and the next day
too as the serpent had its way
again, in those days when young men
ate the heart of any rattler
they killed raw, to give them courage,
to make them brave against the wear
of time, snake blood soaring in their own.

Mountain Dulcimer

Where does such sadness in wood come
from? How could longing live in these
wires? The box looks like the most fragile
coffin tuned for sound. And laid
across the knees of this woman
it looks less like a baby nursed
than some symbolic Pietà,
and the stretched body on her lap
yields modalities of lament
and blood, yields sacrifice and sliding
chants of grief that dance and dance toward
a new measure, a new threshold,
a new instant and new year that
we always celebrate by
remembering the old and by
recalling the lost and honoring
those no longer here to strike these
strings like secrets of the most
satisfying harmonies, as
voices join in sadness and joy
and tell again what we already
know, have always known but forget,
from way back in the farthest cove,
from highest on the peaks of love.

The Grain of Sound

A banjo maker in the mountains,
when looking out for wood to carve
an instrument, will walk among
the trees and knock on trunks. He'll hit
the bark and listen for a note.
A hickory makes the brightest sound;
the poplar has a mellow ease.
But only straightest grain will keep
the purity of tone, the sought-
for depth that makes the licks sparkle.
A banjo has a shining shiver.
Its twangs will glitter like the light
on splashing water, even though
its face is just a drum of hide
of cow, or cat, or even skunk.
The hide will magnify the note,
the sad of honest pain, the chill
blood-song, lament, confession, haunt,
as tree will sing again from root
and vein and sap and twig in wind
and cat will moan as hand plucks nerve,
picks bone and skin and gut and pricks
the heart as blood will answer blood
and love begins to knock along the grain.

Madstone

We hold this seed of polished brick
taken from a deer's belly, smooth
as an eye from tumbling, and stick
it to a mad dog's bite to soothe

the ache and draw out the madness.
Shiny as a little moon with
hair coiled inside the hardness,
the concentrated rock will breathe

venom from a snakebite, and oil
from sores of poison ash and oak.
Some carry one in pocket all
their lives to give them secret luck

and antidote to packsaddle sting
or hornet. A madstone held to
a black widow bite will wring
out the drop of deadly tallow.

But it is sanity the nugget
promises most, a chemical
to counter one madness, one hurt,
with another's, cold, medicinal.

Honey

Only calmness will reassure
the bees to let you rob their hoard.
Any sweat of fear provokes them.
Approach with confidence, and from
the side, not shading their entrance.
And hush smoke gently from the spout
of the pot of rags, for sparks will
anger them. If you go near bees
every day they will know you.
And never jerk or turn so quick
you excite them. If weeds are trimmed
around the hive they have access
and feel free. When they taste your smoke
they fill themselves with honey and
are laden and lazy as you
lift the lid to let in daylight.
No bee full of sweetness wants to
sting. Resist greed. With the top off
you touch the fat gold frames, each cell
a hex perfect as a snowflake,
a sealed relic of sun and time
and roots of many acres fixed
in crystal-tight arrays, in rows
and lattices of sweeter latin
from scattered prose of meadow, woods.